Books in The Tuttle Twins series:

The Tuttle Twins Learn About the Law
The Tuttle Twins and the Miraculous Pencil
The Tuttle Twins and the Creature from Jekyll Island
The Tuttle Twins and the Food Truck Fiasco
The Tuttle Twins and the Road to Surfdom
The Tuttle Twins and the Golden Rule
The Tuttle Twins and the Search for Atlas
The Tuttle Twins and their Spectacular Show Business
The Tuttle Twins and the Fate of the Future
The Tuttle Twins and the Education Vacation
The Tuttle Twins and the Messed Up Market

Find them all at TuttleTwins.com

© 2014 Connor Boyack
All rights reserved.

No graphic, visual, electronic, film, microfilm, tape recording, or any other means may be used to reproduce in any form, without prior written permission of the author, except in the case of brief passages embodied in critical reviews and articles.

ISBN 978-0-9892912-2-4 (paperback)
ISBN 978-1-943521-33-3 (hardback)

Boyack, Connor, author.
The Tuttle Twins Learn About The Law / Connor Boyack.

Cover design by Elijah Stanfield
Edited and typeset by Connor Boyack

Printed in the United States

16 15 14

THE TUTTLE TWINS
Learn About
THE LAW

CONNOR BOYACK

Illustrated by Elijah Stanfield

This book is dedicated to
Frédéric Bastiat (1801-1850).

A great man
with a great mind.

Ethan and Emily Tuttle were happy nine-year-old twins who loved learning new things. They were brother and sister, but they were also good friends. They liked doing things together.

One day in school, their teacher, Mrs. Miner, taught the students about wisdom. Mrs. Miner said that wisdom is when a person knows important and true things.

For their homework, Ethan and Emily had to interview someone who was wise.

They were supposed to ask a wise person to teach them about something very important. Both of them immediately thought of their next door neighbor, Fred.

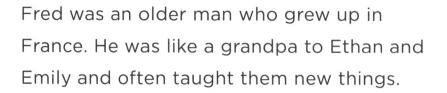

Fred was an older man who grew up in France. He was like a grandpa to Ethan and Emily and often taught them new things.

They enjoyed talking to each other while the twins played in their backyard and Fred worked in his garden.

Fred seemed to know a lot of interesting stuff. The twins could ask Fred almost anything—like how clouds got their different shapes...

or how gasoline makes a car engine run, or how hummingbirds seem to float in the air.

He seemed to have an answer for every question! He would be the perfect person for the interview.

After school, Ethan and Emily dropped their things off at home and hugged their mom. They gathered up some notebooks and pencils, and ran across the lawn to Fred's house.

The twins knocked on his door, and Fred opened it, greeting them with a large grin. "How are my favorite neighbors?" asked Fred.

The twins smiled—they liked being the favorites.

"What can I help you two with today?" Fred asked them.

"We're learning about wisdom in Mrs. Miner's class!" Ethan replied. "We're supposed to interview someone who has it," Emily said.

"I see," said Fred, who chuckled as he realized why they came to him. "And you two think that I can help you?"

"You bet!" Emily said. "Will you help us?" Ethan asked eagerly. "Mrs. Miner said that you should teach us about something very important."

"I can try," Fred said as he turned around. "I think I know just what to talk with you about. Follow me!"

Emily, the more energetic of the twins, leaped through the doorway. Ethan walked in behind her and they followed Fred upstairs to his office.

It was like being in a library, with bookshelves all around the room. There were also extra stacks of overflowing books piled everywhere. Fred clearly liked to read a lot.

"Have a seat, kids," Fred said, pointing to the couch. "I want to help you understand what I think is very important."

Fred reached up high with one hand to pull down a book. "It's something that affects every person every day," he told them.

The Tuttle twins were curious. What could it be, they wondered?

Ethan was very clever and liked trying to figure things out. He asked if it might be something about food, since we all eat every day.

Emily had a creative imagination and had a different idea. "I bet it's about the sun!" she said, trying to guess.

"Those things are important, but I have something else in mind," said Fred.

"What is it?" Ethan asked excitedly. He was getting more curious by the minute.

Fred held out the book he had taken off the shelf. "This!" Fred told them.

Ethan and Emily read the title of the book: *The Law*. They couldn't quite pronounce the author's name, Frédéric Bastiat.

"My parents named me after this man," explained Fred. "He taught people many important ideas about the government."

The twins glanced at each other with a look of confusion on their faces. "The law affects us every day?" Emily asked, looking up at Fred.

"That's what you think is very important?" Ethan asked, folding his arms and furrowing his brow. "Are you sure?" he said while he wrote down "The Law" in his notebook.

"It's absolutely important," Fred said. "And I bet by the time we're done, you'll agree!"

Ethan still wasn't convinced. He was used to learning about interesting things like sharks or Venus flytraps or rockets.

"Our uncle is a police officer," Emily told Fred. "I think he works with the laws."

"Yes, he does," Fred agreed. "When people think of the law, they usually think of speeding tickets or putting criminals in jail. But it's much more than that!" he said.

"You, me, and every other person has something called *rights*," he explained.

Emily wrote "We have rights" in her notebook.

"Having rights means that there are some things I can do, and nobody else is allowed to stop me," Fred explained.

"Like playing with my own toys?" Ethan wondered aloud.

"Sure," Fred said. "Or talking about things you want, or spending time with your friends, or going to church," Fred told them.

"While you two are still children, your parents are responsible to teach you and help you to use your rights in a good way," he said. "But not when I'm all grown up!" Emily said, standing up on her tiptoes to be taller.

"That's right," Fred replied. "As adults, nobody else should stop you from using your rights. You'll be responsible for yourselves."

Ethan wondered what he and Emily would look like as grown ups. What would they do with all of their rights?

"I know you and your family go to church," Fred said. Ethan and Emily nodded. "Think of rights this way. God gives us our lives, and he gives us our ability to think, learn, and act."

"God also gives us the ability to know what things are right or wrong," he told them.

Ethan's eyes lit up. "That's called your conscience!" he said in a loud voice.

RIGHT

WRONG

"That's exactly right, Ethan," Fred told him. He was happy to see that they were beginning to understand.

Ethan wrote "We have a conscience" in his notebook after Fred helped him with the spelling. Emily wrote "Our rights are from God" in hers.

"God gave us these things, and we have the responsibility to preserve and develop them," he said. Fred looked serious when he began to say, "We also need to protect them."

"From bad guys?" Emily asked, as she held her clenched fist in the air.

"Exactly right," Fred replied, smiling. "Since people want to protect their rights and stop the bad guys, they group together. We often call this type of group a government," he said.

Emily and Ethan locked arms and ran around the room punching and kicking the air. "So the government fights the bad guys, right?" Ethan asked. He was imagining government agents in superhero costumes!

"That's the idea, Ethan. But it doesn't always work out that way," Fred told them. "In many cases, the bad guys can become part of the government!"

They stopped punching and kicking. Their jaws dropped open in disbelief. "There are bad guys who are part of the government? How can that be?" wondered Emily.

"Bad guys in government don't wear capes or look like villains," Fred said. "They look normal and say things that a lot of people like," he explained.

Emily wrote "Bad guys can be in government" in her notebook as a reminder.

"If there are bad guys in government, what do they do?" Ethan asked for their next interview question.

"That's an important question, Ethan," noted Fred as he looked out the window. "Let's go out to my garden so I can explain."

It was a sunny afternoon and the breeze felt wonderful. Ethan always liked exploring new things in the outdoors. Emily liked chasing butterflies and birds.

Fred led them over to the raised garden boxes he worked in each day.

He was growing tomatoes, corn, peppers, and zucchini, among other things.

"Do you see my prized tomatoes here?" Fred asked. "Mrs. Lopez across the street really enjoys these whenever I take her some."

Fred plucked a juicy, red tomato off of its vine, and held it out toward the twins. "What would you think if she were to take one of my tomatoes without asking?" he questioned.

"Well, that would be wrong, of course," said Emily matter-of-factly. Their parents had always taught them that stealing was wrong.

"Shouldn't her conscience tell her to stop?" Ethan thought out loud.

"Definitely," Fred replied.

"Now imagine that Mrs. Lopez asks your police officer uncle to help her get one. What would you think if he came and took my tomatoes to give to Mrs. Lopez?"

Ethan suspected that this was a trick question. "That would still be wrong," he said cautiously.

"Even if it was somebody from the government doing it for her?" he asked Emily.

"Wrong is wrong, no matter who does it!" she simply said.

"That's exactly right," Fred proudly replied.

Ethan wrote down "Stealing is always wrong."

"You two are learning something that many people don't understand," he said. "Remember how we all have rights? And that we form governments to protect those rights?"

"Yep," Emily said as she interlocked arms with her brother, ready to fight the bad guys.

"If something is wrong for *us* to do, it's wrong for the people in *government* to do," Fred told them. Ethan and Emily both nodded. "Wrong is wrong, no matter what!" Emily said.

Fred's cat Dusty had followed the group outside and began to make purring sounds. Ethan patted Dusty and asked "Do bad guys in government take your things, Fred?"

"Let's go into the kitchen so I can explain that," Fred said. The twins raced to be the first inside.

Fred opened the door to his large pantry. It had many shelves full of food. It was like being inside a grocery store!

"I store extra food in here so I can help people who are hungry," said Fred.

Emily liked all the colorful boxes of cereal. Ethan was trying to count how many cans of chili Fred had!

"Sometimes I make meals for families when the dad loses his job, or when the mom has a new baby," Fred told them.

"That seems really nice!" Emily commented.

"But what does it have to do with the government?" asked Ethan.

"Well, nothing," Fred stated. "I help people because I want to. But the government forces me to help people, too."

"Is that really so bad?" Emily asked. "Lots of sick or hungry people need our help, right?"

"Remember my question about your police officer uncle taking my tomatoes for Mrs. Lopez?" Fred responded. The twins nodded. It was always wrong to steal, they remembered.

"Just like that, the bad guys in government take my things and give them to others without my permission. Sometimes they take my things to keep for themselves, or give away to their friends instead of helping the needy," Fred told them.

"They sound like they are pirates!" Ethan said, imagining Fred walking the plank at the point of a sword.

Fred chuckled. "Yes Ethan, pirates steal things—that's called plunder. And if bad guys in government do it, we call that legal plunder."

"And there are laws that let bad guys in government plunder like pirates?" Emily asked.

"If a law lets the government do something I'm not allowed to do, then it's not a true law," Fred said.

"True laws protect people and their property from plunder," Fred explained. "When true laws exist and are respected, people work hard to improve their lives and they work peacefully with others. Everyone prospers together and is happier."

Ethan wrote down "True laws protect people."

Fred continued, "When there isn't any legal plunder, people rely on the kindness and service of others for the things that they need."

"But when the law lets people plunder, it turns everyone against each other," Fred said.

"Everyone wants to take instead of give. Some people stop working hard and begin looking to the government to take care of them instead. When this happens, the government begins to control everything."

"They like to control things." Fred told the twins.

"Then who stops the bad guys if they are in the government?" Emily wondered aloud.

"Excellent question!" Fred said, snapping his fingers. "Let's head back upstairs for the answer."

Fred walked back to his office and picked up his copy of *The Law* again. "When the government does bad things, it's hard to fight back because they are very powerful," Fred said. "Being bullied by a kid at school is bad, but imagine if all the teachers and the principal were bullies," he continued.

"I would probably run away from school!" Ethan replied. "So would I," agreed Fred. He handed the book to his interviewers.

"And so we fight back with ideas," said Fred. "Like the ones in this book. Like the ones I've been teaching you about just now."

"Remember that you two are special," he told the twins. "You have rights, and so you also have responsibilities. You should help people if they need something, but the law shouldn't force you to."

Emily wrote "We should help people" in her notebook. "That makes sense," she said. "But why don't more people know about it?"

"That's what wisdom is all about, Emily. We each have to learn important lessons that we use in our lives, and then teach to others," Fred said.

"That's what books like this help us do," he told the twins, pointing to the copy of *The Law* they were still holding.

"It's what wise people throughout history have done. And now you can help your friends and family learn about it, too!" Fred suggested.

Fred said they could borrow his book, even though they didn't know a lot of the words in it. "Maybe your parents would enjoy reading it," he told them.

He also gave them a jar of his prized tomatoes to take home.

As they were walking back to their home, Ethan had a great idea and suddenly stopped. He whispered his idea to Emily, who smiled and nodded. The twins had a plan!

Looking both ways first, they crossed the street and knocked on the door of a nearby house. Mrs. Lopez opened the door, happy to see the twins.

"We brought you a present, Mrs. Lopez!" Ethan and Emily said in unison. They handed the prized tomatoes to her with smiles from ear to ear.

"We wanted to share with you, and nobody else made us do it," Ethan explained.

"You Tuttle twins are very kind, and wise beyond your years!" Mrs. Lopez said.

To thank them for their good deed, she offered them each a homemade cookie. They felt happy that they had learned some wisdom that day.

The End

The Author

Connor Boyack is president of Libertas Institute, a free market think tank in Utah. In that capacity he has changed a significant number of laws in favor of personal freedom and free markets, and has launched a variety of educational projects, including The Tuttle Twins children's book series. Connor is the author of over a dozen books.

A California native and Brigham Young University graduate, Connor currently resides in Lehi, Utah, with his wife and two children.

The Illustrator

Elijah Stanfield is owner of Red House Motion Imaging, a media production company in Washington.

A longtime student of Austrian economics, history, and the classical liberal philosophy, Elijah has dedicated much of his time and energy to promoting the ideas of free markets and individual liberty. Some of his more notable works include producing eight videos in support of Ron Paul's 2012 presidential candidacy. He currently resides in Richland, Washington, with his wife April and their six children.

Contact us at TuttleTwins.com!

Hi, parents!

My name is Frédéric Bastiat, and what your kids just read is a simplified version of my book, *The Law*.

I wrote the book in 1850, but believe that the principles it contains are as relevant to your day as they were to mine—if not more so!

In *The Law* I describe what the proper role of government is, and what true laws are. If you like liberty or limited government, then you'll love my book!

Here are a few select quotes to give you an idea of what you'll find in the brief book:

Want to learn more?
Scan this QR code or visit
LibertasUtah.org/thelaw

"Life, liberty, and property do not exist because men have made laws. On the contrary, it was the fact that life, liberty, and property existed beforehand that caused men to make laws in the first place."

"But how is this legal plunder to be identified? Quite simply. See if the law takes from some persons what belongs to them and gives it to other persons to whom it does not belong. See if the law benefits one citizen at the expense of another by doing what the citizen himself cannot do without committing a crime."

"As long as it is admitted that the law may be diverted from its true purpose—that it may violate property instead of protecting it— then everyone will want to participate in making the law, either to protect himself against plunder or to use it for plunder."

"If the natural tendencies of mankind are so bad that it is not safe to permit people to be free, how is it that the tendencies of these organizers are always good? Do not the legislators and their appointed agents also belong to the human race? Or do they believe that they themselves are made of a finer clay than the rest of mankind?"

Get your own copy or buy them in bulk for **only $1 each!**

Glossary of Terms

Conscience: An inner voice or feeling guiding you to know and do what is right.

Law: A system of rules that are established and enforced to govern a person's behavior.

Plunder: Stealing property from another person.

Right: An entitlement to have, do, or believe something that nobody can take away from you.

Wisdom: The quality of having knowledge, experience, and good judgment.

Discussion Questions

1. Why is it important to listen to your conscience?
2. Is it always wrong to take something from another person without their permission?
3. What rights do you have?
4. If bad guys can be in the government, how can we know who they are? And when we know who they are, what can we do about it?
5. What are some examples of "laws" that allow for the government to plunder us?
6. What are some examples of "true laws" that protect us?

Don't Forget the Activity Workbook!

Visit **TuttleTwins.com/LawWorkbook** to download the PDF and provide your children with all sorts of activities to reinforce the lessons they learned in the book!